Faithfulness
in Our Day-to-Day Life

Faithfulness
in Our Day-to-Day Life

by

Chandrakumar Manickam

Hope Publishing House
Pasadena, California

Copyright 2013 Hope Publishing House

All rights reserved.

For information address:

Hope Publishing House
P.O. Box 60008
Pasadena, CA 91116 - U.S.A.
Tel: (626) 792-6123 / Fax: (626) 792-2121
E-mail: hopepub@sbcglobal.net
Web site: http://www.hope-pub.com

Printed on acid-free paper

Cover design — Michael McClary/The Workshop

Library of Congress Cataloging-in-Publication Data

Manickam, Chandrakumar.
Faithfulness in our day-to-day life/by
Chandrakumar Manickam.
- 1st edition
    p. cm.
ISBN 978-1-932717-28-0 (trade pbk. : alk. paper)
1. Loyalty—Religious aspects—Christianity.
2. Faith. I. Title.
BV4647.L6M36   2013
248.4—dc23

                                            2013022245

I dedicate this book to my dear wife, SARA KASTHURI, who has always stood by me in full cooperation—in order that together we might live faithful, uncompromising lives, pleasing to the Lord.

Other books by the author:

Change Your Tomorrow by Your Action Today

Leadership Insights from Heroes of the Bible

Wedlock or Deadlock?

Exercise Spiritual Authority

Which Way Lord?

Enoch — A Humble, Honest and Holy Walk with God

Are You Ready? Jesus Is Coming Soon

Overcoming Temptation

Who Are You? Where Are You Going?

Seed of the Woman

How to Dig Deep into the Bible?

Foreword

Probably the most important word for faithfulness in Christian living is commitment.

Commitment for the Christian primarily means to the person of our Lord Jesus Christ. But commitment also entails a program because our Lord Jesus Christ came to announce the kingdom of God. So for us Christians, commitment is also to the kingdom of God.

The kingdom for Christians is not in abstract terms—it encompasses concrete relationships. But commitment for the Christian is to other human beings. So our commitment to the Lord Jesus Christ, to the kingdom of God and to other human beings cannot be expressed without the proper use of all the means within our control as Christians. Hence, in this very remarkably terse effort, Dr. Chandrakumar has attempted to describe faithfulness in Christian living in all these contexts.

There is an element about faithfulness that we dare not overlook. Someone said, "Talent attracts talent," which is tantamount to saying, "Like begets like." Nothing can be compared to the faithfulness in other people around us. Somehow, those who have maintained a commitment to the Lord and to God's kingdom and the people around them, evoke in all those who have contact with them a similar nature or quality.

John Newton, the famous composer of the hymn, "Amazing Grace" was one such person. In 1785, while he was the distinguished pastor of St. Mary Woolnoth in London, he drew the attention of William Wilberforce, the young and brilliant politician. At the time Wilberforce was only 26, but already a member of the parliament and his colleagues predicted a great political career for him.

Wilberforce, who had recently experienced a religious awakening and now "reborn," sought out the 64-year-old Newton for counsel. He wanted to know if he should resign from Parliament and enter the ministry. Newton advised him to remain where he was in politics. "God can make you a blessing, both as a Christian and as a statesman."

Still, young Wilberforce was looking for a cause and Newton preached against slavery. This seemed too costly for any political party to dare touch—but it was also a cause no true Christian could evade.

Newton then told him of his personal experience. Years before he had been sailing to and from Africa—a broken man who had command of a slave ship. It was from this history of degradation that he had tasted "Amazing Grace." He came back to England to address the Privy Council, which included Prime Minister William Pitt explaining to them how "the slaves lie in two rows, one above the other, on each side of the ship, like books upon a shelf. The poor creatures are in irons, both hands and feet. And every morning in more instances than one are found the living and the dead fastened together."

In March 1807, Parliament passed the Wilberforce Bill abolishing slavery. And on December 21, 1807, the Rev. John Newton, then 82 years old, spoke his last words,

"I am a great sinner and Christ is a great Savior."

Faithfulness in one produces faithfulness in another. The chain is unending.

May such history-making, history-changing, faithfulness emerge in the heart and life of every reader of this book so that the great contagion of faithfulness might spread across the nations in the hearts and lives of every true believer.

And may the Lord grant it so! Hallelujah.

—Rev. Dr. Samuel Kamaleson

World Vision International

Introduction

We live in an era of compromise. Very few are faithful in fulfilling their God-given responsibilities. Through our lives we follow the path of least resistance. We hold on to a conviction only until it gets in the way of our comfort. We maintain a standard as long as it does not hinder something we wish to do. Sometimes we ignore the principles we claim to follow in order to accomplish our selfish goals. Such a self-centered, worldly perspective is so widespread that we essentially live in a world of compromise. Hence we are going to discuss in this book how we can live an uncompromising, faithful Christian life.

What is Faithfulness?

The Greek word for faithfulness is *pistos* which means trustworthiness, reliability and confidence.

Faithfulness is an attribute or quality applied in the Bible to both God and to people. When used of God, it has in the Old Testament a two-fold emphasis, referring first to God's absolute reliability, firm constancy and complete freedom from arbitrariness or fickleness and secondly to the Lord's steadfast, loyal love toward his people and God's loyalty. He is faithful in keeping his promises and is therefore worthy of trust. When used of humans, the Bible exhorts us to be faithful in fulfilling our God-given responsibilities and to be loyal to the Lord.

Contents

Author's Note

I thank God not only for motivating me but also for enabling me to write this book at this most needed hour. We live in an era of compromise. As I travel around this world I find that very few Christians are faithful in fulfilling their God-given responsibilities. There has been a tremendous response to this message wherever I have preached it at pastors' and Christian leaders' conferences. Hence it is my sincere prayer that the contents of this book may inspire and motivate all believers in our Lord Jesus not to be compromisers but rather overcomers through Christ who strengthens us.

—Prof. Dr. Chandrakumar Manickam

1

Faithfulness in Thoughts and Words

Above all else, God expects us to be faithful in our private life. This is most important and highly essential. If we are not faithful to God in our inward life, we cannot be faithful to God in our public life.

Our Lord Jesus made it quite clear to James and John that the highest positions in a public venue are reserved for those who have qualified in secret—in their private lives. Thus God expects us to be faithful to the Lord in our thoughts, words, motives, actions and in our relationships with one another.

1. Faithful in Our Thoughts

Regarding our thought life, Scripture gives us the order established in Romans 1:21-32. Verse 21 tells us, "For even though they knew God, they did not honor Him as God or give thanks, but they became futile in their speculations, and their foolish heart was darkened."

Even though it is clear that these individuals knew God, they had become vain in their reasoning, or in other words they had become arrogant in their thought life. Verse 22 goes on to explain just what happens at this point: "Professing to be wise, they became fools."

This "professing" took place internally in their thoughts

and this then produced the external action described in verse 23: "And exchanged the glory of the incorruptible God for an image in the form of corruptible man and of birds and four-footed animals and crawling creatures."

The next verse describes the horrible consequences of such choices: "Therefore God gave them over in the lusts of their hearts to impurity, so that their bodies would be dishonored among them."

We thus see the progression: What started as an idea in their thought life resulted in external behavior which was followed by the consequences of this action. If we are faithful, truthful, sincere and open to the conviction and correction of the Holy Spirit of God in our internal thought life, then the external result will be a true spiritual life. Moral or spiritual battles are not won in the external world first. They are always a result—flowing naturally from a cause—and the cause is in the internal world of one's thoughts.

Emphasizing this fact with a great force, Jesus said, "You brood of vipers, how can you, being evil, speak what is good? For the mouth speaks out of that which fills the heart" (Mt. 12:34). Later he explains: "It is not what enters into the mouth that defiles the man, but what proceeds out of the mouth, this defiles the man" (Mt. 15:11).

Here again it is the inward action that Jesus stresses. The internal comes before the external and what is inside produces the behavior that comes out. It is simply a matter of cause and effect.

Even in the Sermon on the Mount, Jesus emphasizes

this aspect when he explains, "Everyone who is angry with his brother shall be guilty before the court" (Mt. 5:22). Compare this with 1 John 3:15, "Everyone who hates his brother is a murderer." Jesus expounded on how guilty our thought lives make us when he said in Matthew 5:28 that, "everyone who looks at a woman with lust for her has already committed adultery with her in his heart."

So in our thought lives we can be deadly sinners, and be equally condemned and liable to be dealt with severely by our righteous Judge. Thus we are totally accountable to God for the thoughts that we think and must exercise self-control in order to keep our thoughts pure and clean, allowing us to be inwardly faithful to the Lord.

2. Faithful in Words

We must also be faithful to the Lord with our spoken words. Is the language that emerges from lips true to our conscience? Sometimes the actual truth is far away from the words that we utter. We even sometimes try to conceal the bitterness in our hearts towards others by speaking to them with sugar-coated words.

The Psalmist says that a wicked person's words are smoother than butter, but there is war in his heart, and though his words sound as soothing as oil, in actuality they cut like sharp swords (55:21).

In Proverbs 10:18 we read: "He who conceals hatred has lying lips." So do we have lying lips? "Lying lips are an abomination to the Lord, but those who deal faithfully are His delight" (Prov. 12:22). The previous verses make clear that the word "faithful" here means our faithfulness in our word life: "Truthful lips will be established forever, but a lying tongue is only for a moment" (v. 19).

The Word of God consistently warns us severely against lying. Nowhere in Scripture do we find a delineation between such a thing as a "black lie," "red lie" or "white lie." A lie IS a lie! "Do not lie to one another, since you laid aside the old self with its evil practices" (Col. 3:9).

It is an evil practice. We read in Revelation 21:8, "But for the cowardly and unbelieving and abominable and murderers and immoral persons and sorcerers and idolaters and all liars, their part will be in the lake that burns with fire and brimstone, which is the second death."

It is clear from Scriptures that liars are compared equally with murderers and immoral persons. "Nothing unclean, and no one who practices abomination and lying, shall ever come into [heaven] (Rev. 21:27). Outside heaven would be "the dogs and the sorcerers and the immoral persons and the murderers and the idolaters, and everyone who loves and practices lying" (Rev. 22:15).

We read in Revelation 14:4-5 about the 144,000 witnesses: "These are the ones who follow the Lamb wherever He goes ... and no lie was found in their mouth; they are blameless."

So, let us have the fear of the Lord in our word-life, for every word we speak we will need to give an accounting to the Lord. As Jesus said, "But I tell you that every careless word that people speak, they shall give an accounting for it in the day of judgment" (Mt. 12:36-37).

The Epistles emphasize this directive: "Do not let any unwholesome talk come out of your mouths, but only what is helpful for building others up according to their needs, that it may benefit those who listen" (Eph. 4:29 NIV). Paul also charged Christ's followers: "Let your speech always be with grace, as though seasoned with salt, so that you will know how you should respond to each person" (Col. 4:6).

"Every man has a right to be wrong in his opinions, but no man has a right to be wrong in his facts."

—Bernard M. Baruch

Faithfulness in Our Day-to-Day Life

2

Faithfulness in Motives and Actions

In our private lives we also must be faithful to the Lord in both our motives and our actions. Everything we do, everything we perform comes from certain actions with certain motives. But there is a great possibility that we can do the right things, but from the wrong motives. Sometimes we can help or support others or be good or talk nicely to them with a sincerely wrong motive looking for some personal security or personal gain.

Even God clarifies His motives before taking any action. That is why the Lord explains to the people of Israel, "I had concern for My holy name... Therefore,... it is not for your sake, O house of Israel, that I am about to act, but for My holy name, which you have profaned among the nations where you went" (Ezk. 36:21-23).

The Psalmist also tells us that God saved the people of Israel for His name's sake and to make His mighty power known (106:8).

Jesus said, "Beware of practicing your righteousness before men to be noticed by them; otherwise you have no reward with your Father who is in heaven. So when you give to the poor, do not sound a trumpet before you, as the hypocrites do in the synagogues and in the streets, so that they may be honored by men. Truly I say to you, they have their reward in full. But when you give to the poor, do not let your left hand know what your right hand is doing, so that your giving will be in secret.... When you pray, you are not to be like the hypocrites; for they love to stand and pray in the synagogues and on the street corners so that they may be seen by men.... [Then] your Father who sees what is done in secret will reward you" (Mt. 6:1-6).

For this reason we have to be extremely careful in discerning just what our motives are and should always be critical of our motives, keeping them open to the correction and conviction of the Holy Spirit of God.

3

Faithfulness in Money Matters

We must be faithful to God in our Penny Life as well as with our larger money matters. Since childhood we have heard it said that "money talks."

Ray O. Jones, the author of *Top Sacred: Spiritual Ideas in Down-to-Earth Language*, tells us of what a dollar or a rupee note would say: "You hold me in your hand and call me yours. Yet may I not as well call you mine. See, how easily I rule you. To gain me, you would all but die. I am impersonal as rain, essential as water. Without me, men and institutions would die, yet I do not hold the power of life for them; I am futile without the stamp of your desire. I go nowhere unless you send me. I keep strange company. For me, men mock, love and scorn character. Yet I am appointed to the service of saints, to give education to the growing mind and food to the starving bodies of the poor. My power is terrific. Handle me carefully and wisely, lest you become my servant rather than I yours."

John D. Rockefeller also noted, "The poorest person 1 know is the one who has nothing but money."

The Norwegian playwright Henrik Ibsen said, "Money may be the husk of many things, but not the kernel. It brings you food, but not appetite; medicine, but not health; acquaintances, but not friends; servants, but not loyalty; days of joy, but not peace or happiness."

These comments are all summed up in Jesus' words: "Beware, and be on your guard against every form of greed; for not even when one has an abundance does his life consist of his possessions" (Lk. 12:15).

Riches are like salt water—the more you drink the more you thirst.

It is good for all who would call themselves Christians to dwell on the mind of Christ in these matters, to think as He thought, and to feel just as He felt about wealth. In this world money is the standard of value. The world loves it, seeks it above everything and often worships it. It is the standard of value not only for material things, but also for people themselves, as they are too often valued according to how much money they possess.

Not only in the kingdom of this world, but also in the kingdom of heaven too, a person is judged by their wealth— but on a much different principle.

The world asks, What does a person own? Christ asks how does that person use it? The world is concerned about getting money, but Christ is concerned about giving money. The world asks, What does that person give? Christ asks, How does that person give? The world looks at the amount of money involved; Christ looks at people and their motives.

This is clearly spelled out in the story of Christ's observing the value of the "two small copper coins" offered to the temple treasury by the poor widow (Mk. 12:41-44). He watched the many rich people donating "large sums" to the temple's coffers, and observed that this was, "out of their surplus;" out of their abundance which meant there

Faithfulness in Our Day-to-Day Life

was no real sacrifice made. Since their life would remain as easy and comfortable as ever, their gifts cost them nothing. In the face of this, Christ notes the poor widow who cast in all that she had, even all her living.

Even King David knew better. When he wanted to buy land to build an altar to the Lord, a plot was offered free of charge to him, but he refused and said, "I will not offer burnt offerings to the Lord my God which cost me nothing" (2 Sam. 24:24).

The world asks how much a person gives? Christ asks how much do they keep? The world looks at the gift. Christ asks whether the gift was a sacrifice. The widow's gift won the heart of Christ and the Lord's approval, for it was in the spirit of His own self-sacrifice, who being rich, became poor for our sakes.

We need to be faithful in our giving. Money given in the spirit of self-sacrifice and love and faith in the One who has paid the full penalty for our sins, brings a rich and eternal reward.

When the Holy Spirit of God came down at Pentecost to dwell in men, He assumed charge and control of their whole life. He took charge of their pennies, as well. He taught them about giving to the church and sharing with one another. He also tested their internal motives in their giving.

The awesome story of Ananias and Saphira has been recounted down through the ages to explain how seriously God looks on the motives of our giving. When these two sold some property they colluded with each other in keeping back a part of the sales price. Yet when Ananias brought the remaining portion and laid it at the feet of the apostles he claimed he was giving them the sum total of the sale.

Both of them were smitten dead by God. Why did this happen? Not because they were unfaithful in their giving, did they die. It was not the question of whether they gave all that they possessed, but whether they gave all that they professed.

The tragedy recounted for us in the Acts of the Apostles (5:1-11) was that both husband and wife plotted this affair and joined hands to lie—not against men but against the Holy Spirit of God. We must never forget that God does not countenance impurity.

A Russian proverb says, "When money speaks, the truth is silent." We must be truthful in all our money matters and give correct accounts even in our totally secular jobs.

Robert Frost humorously said,

> *Never ask of money spent,*
> *Where the spender thinks it went.*
> *Nobody was ever meant,*
> *To remember or invent*
> *What he did with every cent.*

So, every faithful Christian should be faithful in their Penny Life, since we all have to give account to God for every cent we receive and spend.

You can't take your money to heaven, but you can make an investment for eternity. Some people have plenty to live on, but nothing to live for.

4

Faithfulness of Christian Minorities in the Dark Ages

We must be faithful to the Lord even in the midst of persecution.

When our Lord Jesus was pleased to take upon Himself the form of a servant and go about preaching the kingdom of God, He took every opportunity to forewarn His disciples of the many distresses, afflictions and persecutions they must expect to endure for His name's sake.

The apostle Paul, following in the steps of our Lord, was particularly careful to warn young Timothy of the difficulties he must expect to meet within the course of his ministry.

Though all followers of Christ face persecution, yet it may be in differing degrees. All Christians will find by their own experience that whether they act in a private or public capacity, they must in some degree or other suffer persecution.

Not all who are persecuted are real Christians, for many sometimes suffer and are persecuted for having done wrong rather than for righteousness sake. The most important question is: Are you still faithful to God in spite of being persecuted for godly living?

It is estimated that more than 50 million Christians

died for their faith in the Dark Ages. A million Christians died for their faith when the Communists seized China; innumerable thousands died as martyrs in Africa—and so the story goes on and on throughout the history of Christendom.

1. Why should we expect persecution?

(i) First, because our Lord promised blessings would follow to all who suffer for Christ, as we read in Matthew's gospel: "Blessed are those who have been persecuted for the sake of righteousness" (5.10).

(ii) Second, because our Lord Himself experienced it. When you follow the footsteps of our Lord from the manger to the cross and compare this to whatever persecution we might have borne, it immediately is apparent that nothing like what our Lord went through while He was on the planet earth has been any of our lots. The Son of God was hated by wicked men, reviled, counted amongst the outcasts and called a blasphemer, a drunkard, a Samaritan, and a devil. Our Lord was stoned, thrust out of synagogues, called a deceiver of people, and treated as a base enemy— scourged by Caesar, spit upon, condemned and nailed to an accursed tree by insolent guards and left to die in agony.

(iii) Third, because the saints of all ages have experienced persecution and continue to this day to face it. From the time that Abel was made a martyr for practicing his religion through the telling of how the son of the bondwoman mocked Isaac up until the present day we hear stories of those who suffered for their faith. As for Christ's followers, the Acts of the Apostles make clear that the early Christians were threatened, stoned, imprisoned, scourged and martyred. Even today many saints in all parts of the world are facing severe persecutions.

(iv) Fourth, because of the sinner's enmity against God those who walk the path of holiness are treated as enemies. Wicked men hate God and therefore cannot but hate those who are godly.

(v) Fifth, because according to Scriptures the godly are strengthened in their faith by persecution. To explain why the godly should suffer and be persecuted, the Apostle Paul in his letter to the Corinthians lifts the veil on his private life and allows us to catch a glimpse of his human frailties and needs. He clearly records the specifics of his anguish, tears, affliction and satanic opposition—with details of his persecution, loneliness, imprisonments, beatings, feelings of despair, hunger, shipwrecks, sleepless nights and that "thorn in the flesh"—his companion of pain. It makes us feel close to him as we picture him as an ordinary man with down-to-earth problems we can relate to over the centuries.

Paul gives us three rationales for our suffering and persecution in the first chapter of 2 Corinthians:

a. "So that we will be able to comfort those who are in any affliction" (v. 4). God allows us to suffer so we can develop the capacity to enter into the sorrows and tribulations of others. If you have suffered the loss of your husband or your wife or your child, you can be in complete sympathy with someone else who is going through a similar loss. We are able better to understand their situation having passed through the same deep waters.

b. "So that we would not trust in ourselves" (v. 9). God also allows suffering and persecution in our lives so we might learn what it means to depend on Him, not on our own strength and resources. Repeatedly the Lord reminds us of the consequences of pride, but sometimes only through suffering do we learn the lesson.

c. "So that thanks may be given" (v. 11). God trains us to give thanks in everything. Sometimes, one of the reasons why our suffering is prolonged is that we take so long to say "Thank you, Lord, for this suffering or this experience."

As Charles Swindoll has said, "How unfinished and rebellious and proud and unconcerned we would be without suffering!"

2. What have we endured for the Lord?

Someone wrote about a dream which was quoted in the *Presbyterian Survey* as follows: I saw in a dream that I was in the heavenly and celestial city, though when and how I got there I could not tell. I saw one of a great multitude which no one could number, from all countries and peoples and times and ages. Somehow I found that the saint who stood next to me had been in heaven more than 1,860 years.

"Who are you?" I asked him. (We both spoke the same languages of heavenly Canaan, so we understood one another).

Faithfulness in Our Day-to-Day Life

"I," said he, "was a Roman Christian. I lived in the days of the Apostle Paul and was one of those who died in Nero's persecutions. I was covered with pitch and fastened to a stake and set on fire to light up Nero's gardens."

"How awful," I exclaimed.

"No" he said, "I was glad to do something for Jesus. He died on the cross for me."

The man on the other side of him then spoke. "I have been in Heaven only a few hundred years. I came from an island in the Southern seas—Erromanga. John Williams, a missionary, came and told me about Jesus and I, too, learned to love Him. My fellow countrymen killed the missionary and they caught and bound me. I was beaten until I fainted and they thought I was dead, but I revived. The next day they knocked me on the head, cooked and ate me."

"How terrible," I exclaimed.

"No," he answered, "I was glad to die as a Christian. You see the missionaries had told me that Jesus was scourged and crowned with thorns for me."

Then they both turned to me and asked, "What did you suffer for Christ? Or did you sell what you had so the money could be used to send missionaries like John Williams to tell the heathen about Jesus?"

But I was speechless. And while they both were looking at me with sorrowful eyes, I awoke. It was a dream. But I lay on my soft bed awake for hours, thinking of the money I had wasted on my own pleasures, on my extra clothing and expensive car, plus the many other luxuries of my life and I realized I had wasted a considerable part of my life and my fortune.

In order to escape suffering and persecution—and wanting to live an easy life—I had often compromised with the world's standards. The article concluded with the question: "Dear reader, How about you? Is your life also the same?"

Suffering for Christ's sake should be viewed as a privilege. Nothing great was ever done without much enduring.

Let us learn to pray:

Lord, help me to see the sunshine through the
rain, What I count loss may show how be gain
Help me to sing when I would cry
Knowing that thou art standing by.

What matters if this life is brief?
What matters if I've toil or grief?
I, in my Savior, find relief
Of all my joy, He is the chief.
God reigns! I will be true.

So we need to be faithful in our private life, in our public life, in our penny life, in our priestly calling and in our persecution. Let us totally pour out our lives at the altar and be faithful servants of God. Then we can all join in the prayer of the Auca-Huaorani martyr Jim Elliot, "God, I pray thee, light these idle sticks of my life and may I burn for Thee. Consume my life, my God, for it is Thine. I seek not a long life, but a full one, like you, Lord Jesus."

5

Faithfulness in the Husband-Wife Relationship

In family relationships, there are three words that are almost as powerful as the famous "I Love You." These are: "Maybe you're right."

Marriage is one of the most intimate and difficult of human relationships. It is not to be leaped into, but embarked upon with deliberate and solemn steps. It is infinitely rewarding at its best and unspeakably oppressive at its worst. Faithfulness in family relationships primarily refers to a commitment of one to another.

Let us try to understand this commitment between members of a Christian family.

Deep

Too many people marry for better or worse, but not for good.

When a pastor asked, "Do you take this man for better or worse?" the bride replied, "He can't become any worse or any better, so I take him as he is."

Marriage is a unique human relationship with a deepening and expanding experience. It needs plenty of give and take if it is to survive. If one partner constantly gives while the other only does the taking, then it is a possessive and unhealthy relationship. A satisfying marriage relationship does not come naturally. Both the husband and wife need to faithfully fulfill the unique responsibilities as put forth in the Bible.

Distinct

The Bible places distinct demands upon the husband and his unique role in the marriage. In the Christian family the husband stands as the representative of Christ and is called to love his wife just as Christ loved the church (see Ephesians 5:23-30).

And just how did Christ love the Church? He came from heaven's glory to take on the role of a servant, demonstrating the ultimate form of love—giving of oneself.

Therefore, the husband's love towards his wife is to be expressed in loving service on her behalf, caring for her, as unto weaker vessel (1 Pet. 3:7); rather than demanding and commanding her submission. Husbands must recognize that their wives occupy a place of honor in the home. Every husband should judge his love for his wife nothing less than the sacrifice of his own best interests for her best interests.

Direct

Paul clearly instructs husbands not to be bitter and harsh (Colossians 3:19). They are to respect and honor their wives and feel free to share with them their deepest feelings—without secretly holding anything back to themselves. They must communicate tactfully with their wives, explaining why they are having difficulty, asking for their help and cooperation. They should not judge any failures or attribute wrong actions against them, since love keeps no record of wrongs (1 Corinthians 13:5). And they should involve their wives directly on family matters and issues.

Conflict between husband and wife not only affects the spiritual atmosphere of the home, but their physical health as well. Doctors say that husband—wife fighting can produce rheumatoid arthritis in women because of resentments they internalize, and peptic ulcers in men because of emotional upsets. Issues in the family need to be sorted out through sharing and caring.

Voluntary

Many wives find it difficult either to accept or appreciate the concept of submission as mentioned in Ephesians 5:22, 24; 1 Peter 3:1 and Colossians 3:18. Here Paul and Peter are talking about a voluntary submission, which flows from love and respect for the husband. It is a self-subordination and has nothing to do with individual worth or basic equality. It is her Christian duty and is according to the will of God. The Scripture clearly indicates that this submission is mandatory, not optional, and is to be continuous. It is to be done "as unto the Lord" (Eph. 5:22).

Refusal to submit to the husband is therefore rebellion against God's commands. The wife then must look upon her submission to her husband as an act of love and obedience to Christ and not merely just to her husband (Jn. 14:15).

Complementary

To be more specific, the wife's submission is a spiritual matter because it should be performed in the power of Holy Spirit. The context in which such submission is commanded indicates that it can be performed only by women cleansed by the blood of Christ who have yielded themselves to the total control of the Holy Spirit of God (Eph. 1:1-5:21; 1 Pet. 1:1-3:6). Bill Gothard defines this submission as "the freedom to be creative under divinely appointed authority."

God designed women to be a complementary partner to men (Gen. 2:18). Submission means that she sees herself as a part of her husband's team. She can have her own ideas, opinions, desires, requests and insights, but she should lovingly make them known to her husband because in any good team, the leader makes the final decisions and plans.

Submission does not mean that the wife is inferior to her husband. The Hebrew word for helper in Genesis 2:18 is used in Scriptures often to describe God as being a helper to all of us (Ps. 33:20). Just as God is the head of Christ and yet Christ and God are equals, so it is with husband and wife. Therefore, being a wife is a dignified, responsible and honorable position.

A Christian wife should find her great joy and satisfaction in willing subjection to her husband out of love. The wife's submission should come with a realization that at last her heart has found its rest.

Healthy

The husband and wife should be faithful to each other in thought, words, motives and action. We are accountable to God for any unhealthy thoughts we think about our spouse. Thus we need to discipline ourselves to keep our thoughts pure and clean so that we might share them openly with each other without having any secret thoughts about the other. Are the words that come out of our lips true to our conscience? It is not right to hide bitterness in our hearts towards each other and speak with sugar-coated words. As Proverbs tells us, "He who conceals hatred has lying lips" (10:18).

We must also be faithful to each other in our motives and actions. There is a possibility that we can do the right thing with the wrong motives. Sometimes we can help, support, be good or talk lovingly to each other based on a desire for some personal security or gain. So, we should always judge our motives and keep them open to the conviction and correction of the Holy Spirit of God.

More than in any other sector, the husband and wife must be faithful to each other in sexual thoughts and actions. This is an area where many Christian couples have failed. Marriage is a sacrament of love and grace. This love is sealed by sexuality and sexuality in turn needs this love to function with integrity and trust. Thus their love must guard and keep the spouses loyal and faithful to each other.

Faithfulness in Our Day-to-Day Life

6

Faithfulness in the
Parent-Child Relationship

Five-year-old Susan said to the lady next door, "I don't think Mummy knows how to bring up children because she makes me go to bed when I am not sleepy and wakes me up when I am sleeping."

Little Suresh asked his mother, "Why must I always take a nap when you are tired?"

Rejected by the college of his liking, a young lad angrily told his father, "If you really cared for me you would have pulled some wires."

"I know," replied the father sadly, "To begin with I should have first pulled the wires of the T.V., video, stereo and the telephone."

1. Things That Influence Children

Children cannot immediately or easily understand the motive behind certain of their parents' actions, hence parents should have a heart-to-heart chat with them whenever such matters come up. In this way parents can help them comprehend that their decisions arise out of their love and concern for their well-being.

Children are affected most by what they see and hear at home. If a child lives "with criticism, he learns to condemn; with hostility he learns to fight; with fear, he learns to be apprehensive; with tolerance, he learns to be patient; with encouragement, he learns to be confident; with praise he learns to be appreciative; with acceptance, he learns to love, with honesty he learns what truth is; with fairness, he learns justice; with security, he learns to have faith in himself and those about him" *(Sinai Sentry).*

2. The Responsibility of the Parents

The Bible says, "Fathers, do not provoke your children to anger, but bring them up in the discipline and instruction of the Lord" (Eph. 6:4). It also mandates parents: "Do not exasperate your children, so that they will not lose heart" (Col. 3:21).

David Wilkerson has pointed out that, "Every word and deed of a parent is a fiber woven into the character of a child, which ultimately determines how that child fits into the fabric of society."

A teenaged girl told her friend that she gets "A" graded in French because her parents were born in Paris and they speak French at home. Her friend's reply was, "In that case I should be getting A's in geometry, because my parents are often square and talk in circles."

3. The Role of Christian Parents

Below is a list of what children expect their parents to be:

C — Cheerful, courageous, a churchgoer

H — Hopeful, honest, helpful, hospitable, humble

R — Reverent, responsible, righteous, reliable

I — Industrious, informed, inspiring

S — Sincere, slow to anger, sharing, serene

T — Tolerant, temperate

I — Instrument for God, increasing in grace

A — Alert, appreciative

N — Neighborly, never coveting or gossiping

P — Patient, practical, prayerful life

A — Affectionate, approachable

R — Religious, reasonable, relaxed

E — Enthusiastic, even-tempered

N — Not nudging others, never breaking a promise

T — Trustworthy, thankful, tactful

4. Children Regard Parents as Their Model

A child's concept of God is built on their knowledge of their own earthly parents and their relationship with them. If we want our children to think of God as their Heavenly Father then it is important that as parents we should model our Heavenly Father who:

- is unconditionally loving (Rom. 5:8);
- is patient and repeatedly forgiving (Ps. 103:8);
- is always ready to listen (1 Pet. 3:12);
- provides for the needs of His children (Phil. 4:19);
- provides us with security, comfort and encouragement (Ps. 91:4);
- lives a holy life (Lev. 11:44);

- is prepared to make a personal sacrifice for His children (2 Cor. 8:9);
- is fair, just and punishes with love (Deut. 32:4);
- is steadfast and unwavering (Mal. 3:6);
- teaches and guides (Ps. 32:8);
- desires the best for us and delights in the company, presence and fellowship of His children (Prov. 8:31);
- is slow to speak and slow to anger (Jms. 1:19); and
- speaks the truth in love (Eph. 4:15).

5. Children Demand Your Time

More than anything else children value the time parents spend with them. One percent of the child's time is spent in Sunday school, seven percent is at school while 92 percent is at home. Significant time should be devoted by parents to listening, understanding, helping and guiding children in their daily activities. A sage has said, "If you want your child to have a fruitful future, spend twice as much time with them and half as much money."

Children do not think much of the past or worry about their future, but they are eager to experience and enjoy the present. Many parents claim that everything they are engaged in at present—earning money, saving, and building a house—is to ensure a good future for their children. This attitude fails to understand that children evaluate their parents' love and affection for them in terms of time spent with them today, not on money or material spent or saved for their future.

Children start to roam when parents don't stay home. So parents who tend to concentrate more on the future financial benefits for their children rather than on spending time in bringing them up in the fear of the Lord have skewed values.

Considering the number of divorces that occur in our society today would indicate that more parents are running away from home than are their children.

Our children are the only earthly possessions we can take with us to our glorious heavenly home. Visualize your children as lovely, little two-legged walking computers whom we can program into the Biblical path of life by teaching them the word of God and praying for them. If children are to find the way to God, parents must point the way.

Faithfulness in Our Day-to-Day Life

7

Faithfulness in Pain and Suffering

Paul talks about the credentials of his apostolic commission in 2 Corinthians 11:22-27 where he boasts about his weaknesses and then goes on to proclaim that he delights in his infirmities, in the reproaches he has received, in the persecutions he has undergone and in all his distressing circumstances—for the sake of Christ.

He further elaborates about the thorn in his flesh in the following chapter. There have been many conjectures about the identity of this "splinter in the flesh," but whatever it might have been, many have linked it to the "bodily ailment" he spoke of suffering on his first visit to the Galatians.

The answer the apostle received from the Lord for his thrice-repeated prayer for the removal of this sickness was not his deliverance from it, but rather receiving the necessary grace

to bear it—not simply living with the "splinter," but have the grace to be thankful for it. The obvious conclusion from this trial was that ministry was so effective in spite of this physical weakness. The transcendent power was not his own, but from God.

1. Our Weakness Is Essential for God's Power

We need to recognize that our weaknesses are not barriers to God's power, but instead they encourage us to look for ways to avail that power. Paul said, "I will boast of what pertains to my weakness" (2 Cor. 11:30).

Our weaknesses open the way for us to experience the superabundant strength of God's grace. It is from God that we receive the strength to bear our afflictions. When we feel strong in our own might, sometimes we hinder God's power. So in a way, our weakness is essential for God's power to work in us.

But we must also acknowledge that Paul did not glory in the infirmities themselves, but only because through his infirmities Christ had the opportunity to manifest His power more effectively. Paul could rejoice in his personal weakness—in deprivations of food, drink and resources, in persecutions and in all the troubles related to his ministry— because he had the assurance that the grace of God was operating through him.

For this reason Paul had a healthy attitude towards life. Cheerfully he pressed forward toward the goal of his apostolic calling (Phil. 3:12).

The fact that Paul's "thorn in the flesh" was not removed does not mean God cannot or will not heal those who call on Him, nor does it mean that He will necessarily send suffering to those He calls to serve Him. He deals with each person on an individual basis. He will make His grace sufficient for us. Our weaknesses are not handicaps in our service; they are vehicles of God's loving sufficiency.

God proved to Paul that no matter what his own weaknesses were, God's strength was all that was necessary for him to carry out his ministry.

Someone once asked a humble Christian woman, rich toward God, "Are you the woman with the great faith?"

"Oh, no," said replied, "I am the woman with a little faith in a great God!"

2. Knocked down, but Never Knocked out

Paul talks abotit receiving 39 lashes from the Jews five different times in 2 Corinthians 11:24. According to their written law, the maximum number allowed was 40 lashes (Deut. 25:3). On the principle of "setting a hedge around the law" to prevent its accidental transgression, it was traditionally restricted to 39 lashes *(Mishnah Makkot 3:10-15)*.

Three times Paul relates he was beaten with rods. In the Lystra riot Paul was badly knocked about and later he told his friends in Corinth of being stoned once (2 Cor. 11:25). He must have been knocked unconscious, for those who stoned him dragged him out of the city, assuming he was dead. As the new converts gathered around to see what they should do with his body, he regained consciousness and returned back to the city with them (Acts 14:19-20).

Whatever his physical disabilities were, Paul either had an extraordinarily tough and resilient constitution and remarkable staying power or was repeatedly healed miraculously. He was often "struck down, but never destroyed" (2 Cor. 4:9). He speaks of bearing in his body the marks of Jesus—the stigmata which indicated who his master was, just as slaves sometimes had their owner's name branded in their flesh (Gal. 6:17).

3. Paul's Theology of Pain and Suffering

Paul's theology was not based on experiences which might be described as mystical, rather it was based on Jesus, the fulfiller of God's promise and purpose of salvation; Jesus, the crucified and exalted Lord; Jesus, the divine wisdom in whom God creates, maintains and brings to consummation everything that exists; Jesus, who here and now lives within his people by His spirit.

Paul was thrust into the Lord's ministry with a promise of suffering and not with the promise of an easy life. He admitted, "the Holy Spirit solemnly testifies to me in every city, saying that bonds and afflictions await me" (Acts 20:23). Three times he was shipwrecked, spending a night and a day in the deep.

No one can live a Christian life without suffering. Should any so-called Christians come to me and claim they have no problems whatsoever, then I would have the problem of believing they are Christians. There is something basically wrong in the too comfortable life. Such "Christians" must be compromisers, not overcomers.

As sinners we are called to be saved. As saints we are called to suffer. "But if anyone suffers as a Christian, he is not to be ashamed, but is to glorify God in this name" (1 Pet. 4:16). Christ always associated His sufferings and His glorification together.

Without the Cross, there is no Crown. Cross-bearing ends in being Crown-wearing.

Jesus was pierced through for our transgressions. He

was crushed for our iniquities; the chastening for our well-being fell upon him. "Surely our griefs He Himself bore, and our sorrows He carried" (Is. 53:4).

During the war in London, a pastor walking along the street said to a wounded British soldier, "Thank you for being wounded for me," and then further added, "I know someone who was wounded for you."

Jesus, emptied Himself, suffered for us and endured to the extent of a shameful, painful death on the cross for our sake. Is it not our responsibility to honor His sufferings and be willing and ready to suffer for His cause? That is what Paul says in Philippians 3:7-8,10 "I have counted as loss for the sake of Christ.... So that I may gain Christ;... that I may know Him and the power of His resurrection and the fellowship of His sufferings, being conformed to His death."

When we have left this life, we shall not have a second chance of bearing the cross of Christ —*Sadhu Sunder Singh.*

4. In the Storms of Life

Paul's long list of problems and suffering speaks of the struggle in which he had been engaged in order to carry the Gospel of Christ to the world. He actually accepted hardships as normal experiences, rather than as anything out of the ordinary (2 Cor. 11:23-33).

"Labors" (v. 23) probably refers to the physical work he did in order to support himself. "Beaten times without number" speak of the stripes he received as a violator of the Jewish law. Five of his "imprisonments" are recorded in Acts. The three shipwrecks were probably part of his being "often in danger of death." Paul traveled almost constantly putting himself often in danger of floods and robbers and other perils of his time.

What to Do When the Ship Is Sinking?

Jesus was sleeping when the ship with the disciples on it was sinking. A great windstorm arose, and the waves beat into the boat, so that it was already filling. But Jesus was in the stern, asleep on a cushion. When they awoke Him in panic, they exclaimed, "'Teacher, do You not care that we are perishing?' And He got up and rebuked the wind and said to the sea, 'Hush, be still!' And the wind died down and it became perfectly calm. And he said to them, 'Why are you afraid? Do you still have no faith?' They became very much afraid and said to one another, 'Who then is this, that even the wind and the sea obey Him?'" (Mk. 4:35-41; see also Mt. 8:23-27 & Lk. 8:22-25).

During times of difficulty we can often learn more about the Lord. This was the experience of the disciples. This miracle illustrates the truth that even the disciples of Christ went through difficult situations that caused them fear and anxiety.

Often it is only in the storms of life that believers experience the power of God, for it is that power that takes care of our problems. Sometimes money and experience cannot save us, as in the instance of this storm. Too often we need to come to the end of all human resources before we are willing to experience the power of God.

In this instance, the skill of those expert seamen, their knowledge of the lake and their past experiences as sailors were of no use. In their anxiety, the disciples even questioned whether the Lord cared for them. But he did, and he still does.

This was a lesson implanted that night deep in Peter's psyche, so later he could proclaim to the world, "He cares for you" (1 Pet. 5:7 where the same word for "care" is used as in the accounts of this miracle). What a great comfort it is to know that an all-powerful Savior cares for us with an infinitely gracious love!

Jesus was fast asleep in the midst of dashing waves and a drenching storm. How could He do that? No doubt He was not only a true man, but a man of true faith in His heavenly Father.

David could lie down and sleep when he had enemies wanting to kill him. He says, "I lay down and slept; I awoke, for the Lord sustains me. I will not be afraid of ten thousands of people who have set themselves against me round about" (Ps. 3:5-6). Peter was fast asleep in the dungeons of king Herod till the angel of deliverance woke him up, though he knew that death was awaiting him (Acts 12:6).

There were also dangers created by hostile people. But external perils were not the only problem. Paul also underwent other strains, exhaustion, pains, hunger and thirst, fasting, cold and nakedness. The burden of the churches weighed him down—the heresy of Galatia, the confusion in Thessalonica, the immorality in Corinth. All of these were part of the burdens he carried as he established churches around the Mediterranean world.

This all points out the fact that our distresses are not an indication of God's disfavor. Beyond forgetting how Christ agonized on the cross for our sins, one can never conclude that Paul was out of the will of the Lord when he suffered want (Phil. 4:12). Instead we must always realize that our disappointments are God's appointments.

God has not promised His children physical comfort, material prosperity or freedom from persecution—though we live in a dispensation of grace. He has blessed us with all spiritual blessings (Eph. 1:3) and He has promised to supply all our material need (Phil. 4:19), but physical comfort may not necessarily be our material need. Suffering and difficulty may well be expected to characterize a normal Christian experience.

This condition is what Paul meant when he said that as believers we might expect suffering: "For your sake we are being put to death all day long; we were considered as sheep to be slaughtered" (Rom. 8:36; see also 1 Pet. 1:6-7).

Paul recalls a humiliating experience. "In Damascus the ethnarch under Aretas the king was guarding the city of the Damascenes in order to seize me, and I was let down in a basket through a window in the wall, and so escaped his hands" (2 Cor. 11:32-33).

Paul did not boast of his achievements, nor of the hardships he had willingly suffered for the sake of Christ. The scars that his experiences left, he wore with pride— they were the indelible stigmata that proclaimed him to be the bond slave of the Lord in whose service he had received them.

Jesus was all-human. He suffered pain just as you and I would have. The agony was so great that He even went to the extent of praying, "Father if Thou art willing, remove this cup from Me, yet not My will, but Thine be done."

Don't worry if you are shedding tears today because of your stand for Christ. One day, He will wipe away every tear from your eyes, and there will no longer be any mourning, crying or pain. The first things would have passed away (Rev. 21:4). The Lord God will wipe tears away and will remove the reproach of His people from all the earth. This is the Lord for whom we have waited, let us rejoice and be glad in His salvation (Is. 25:8-9). God shall wipe every tear from your eyes (Rev. 7:16-17).

God will take care of what you go through; but you must take care of how you go through it.

8

Faithfulness in Our Attitudes

An attitude is an emotional and motivational force towards a psychological object. Some times we try to picture attitudes as 'value,' 'belief' or 'opinion,' but attitudes are different from them. Belief is its cognitive base, and action is the cognitive side. In fact, attitude is part of a broad value system. We give value to something depending on our beliefs and our attitudes.

Belief is a thought process which includes a clear perception of value. We form an opinion based on our beliefs and attitudes. But our attitudes keep changing with the onset of new environmental influences.

1. The Nature and Choice of Attitude

Nicolo Paganini, a famous and gifted violinist, was playing a difficult piece of music to a packed audience while a full orchestra surrounded him with magnificent support. Suddenly one string of his violin snapped and hung down from his violin. Though he was shocked and was perspiring, he continued to play the music beautifully.

To the conductor's surprise, a second string broke and in a short time a third one broke. Now there were three limping strings dangling from Nicolo's violin, but still the expert performer completed the difficult composition on the one remaining string, at which point the audience jumped to its feet shouting, "Bravo! Bravo!"

As the applause died down, the violinist asked the audience to take their seats; whereupon he held the violin high for all to see and then signaled to the conductor to begin. The orchestra responded and then Paganini placed the violin beneath his chin and played the final piece on the program with only one string on his instrument. Both the audience and the conductor were awed by this marvelous performance. This can certainly be called an attitude of fortitude. Paganini playing magnificently on one string models for us the kind of perseverance we must develop.

What is perseverance? First of all, it means to take hold; then second, to hold on; and last of all, to never let go. The longer we live, the more we become convinced that life is ten percent what happens to us and ninety percent how we respond to what happens, for we are more than what happens to us.

We should not forget that others are constantly watching us—to see what our reactions are, even more than our actions. Anyone dedicated to God should not react to adversity, but only lovingly respond.

How do we respond to our life situations? We respond as we interpret the meaning of actions upon us.

Dr. Victor Frankel was a bold and courageous Jew who as a prisoner endured years of indignity and humiliation by the Nazis. At the beginning of his trial, he was brought into the courtroom.

His captors had taken away his home and his family, his cherished freedom and his possessions—even his watch and his wedding ring. They had shaved his head and stripped his clothing off his body and then he was interrogated and falsely accused.

Destitute with no resources, he was a helpless pawn in the hands of brutal, prejudiced and sadistic captors. For all practical purposes it appeared as though there was nothing he could do. But suddenly Dr. Frankel realized he still had the power to choose his own attitude. No matter what anyone would ever do to him, regardless of what the future held for him, the attitude of choice was his to make. He could either hold on to his bitter feelings or change them into forgiveness. He could give up to hatred or choose hope with a determination to endure instead of giving into the paralysis of self-pity.

It boiled down to Frankel and one string!

In reality we must admit that we spend more of our time concentrating and fretting over the strings that snap, dangle and pop—the things that cannot be changed—than we pay attention to the string that remains—our choice of attitude.

An attitude can be defined as an organization of interrelated beliefs around a common object or a situation with certain aspects being the focus of attention for some—while others choose something totally different to highlight.

Belief is its cognitive base and action its cognitive side. All beliefs are predisposition to action. Each belief within an attitude organization is conceived to have three components such as cognitive, affective and behavioral.

A cognitive component represents a person's knowledge about what is good or bad, true or false, desirable or undesirable. An affective component takes a positive or a negative position with respect to the object of belief when its validity is seriously questioned, as in an argument. The kind of action a behavioral component leads to is dictated strictly by the content of the belief.

Jastrow has pointed out that the human mind is a belief-seeking rather than a fact-seeking apparatus. Virtually all psychological theories agree that an attitude is not a basic, irreducible element within the personality, but it represents a cluster or syndrome of two or more interrelated elements.

Someone has said, "A person's social behavior is mediated by at least two types of attitudes—one activated by the object, the other by the situation." A person's opinion is a verbal expression of a belief, an attitude or a value. The concept of sentiment is more or less synonymous with attitude.

Certain environmental influences produce certain attitudes and hence these may not remain steady, but change with the development of new environmental influences. This change may take place consciously or unconsciously.

It is imperative we consider the impact of our attitudes towards the complexities of our life situations in the following chapters.

2. Attitude Towards Irritation

We need to consider the reality of our reactions to irritations. Some of our common irritants are traffic jams, long lines, crying babies, misplaced keys, nosy and noisy neighbors, peeling onions, flat tires, all the in-laws and outlaws including mothers-in-law and the daughters-in-law.

The secret of overcoming irritation lies in adjusting. There is a three-fold truth about adjusting:

(i) I can change no one by direct action;

(ii) I can change only myself;

(iii) When I change, others tend to change in response to this.

We can learn a great lesson from the oyster and its pearl. Pearls are the product of pain. For some unknown reason, the shell of the oyster gets pierced and an alien substance, a grain of sand, slips inside. When that foreign irritant enters the shell, all the resources within the tiny, sensitive oyster rush to the spot and begin to release healing fluids that otherwise would have remained idle. By and by the irritant is covered and the pearl heals the wound.

No other gem seems as precious as pearls do—in the history of this world. It is the symbol of stress—a healed wound—a precious, tiny jewel conceived through irritation, born of adversity, nursed by adjustments. Had there been no wounding, no irritating interruption, there could have been no pearl.

Some oysters are never wounded, and those seeking pearls, toss them aside, assigning them as fit only for stew curry. The book of James tells us, "When all kinds of trials crowd into your lives, don't resent them as intruders, but welcome them as friends. Realize that they have come to test your endurance. But let the progress go on until the endurance is fully developed, and you will find you have become men and women of mature character."

You must learn to be patient in stressful situations, otherwise you will become a patient. In order to keep mole hills of tensions from becoming mountains of stress you can develop certain precautionary measures such as:

(i) Allow for a margin of error;

(ii) Put things in perspective;

(iii) Plan for delays;

(iv) think ahead;

(v) be prepared even for the worst and

(vi) live for the moment.

3. Attitude of Blaming Others

This is an aggressive attitude that reacts to circumstances with blame. Most of the time we blame others for our failures and the blunders we have committed. Sometimes we even tend to blame God. Blaming is a system of avoiding responsibility. We have an impulse to blame because it promises an escape. Spiritual growth and maturity comes to a Christian only by owning responsibility and working at resolving it.

We should make no excuses for our failures and look for no escapes from our mistakes. This is precisely the way to minimize our failures and cut down our mistakes. Even if some one else is at fault, the responsibility of a Christian is to kindly and lovingly exhort that person, showing much concern for them and their background and their life situation. The most powerful rebuke is not a loud, negative blast but a quiet, positive model.

Charles R. Swindoll says, "Blame never affirms, it assaults. Blame never restores, it wounds. Blame never solves, it complicates. Blame never unites, it separates. Blame never smiles, it frowns. Blame never forgives, it rejects. Blame never forgets, it remembers. Blame never builds, it destroys."

Let us face the fact that until we stop blaming others, we will not start enjoying health and happiness again. Rather, if we own the mess we are in there is hope for us and we will receive help.

4. Attitude of Rationalization

Rationalization is a dangerous attitude which has corrupted many lives and destroyed many leaders. The dictionary defines rationalizing as, "providing plausible but untrue reasons for conduct." In other words, it is what we do when we substitute untrue explanations for true reasons. One sin rationalized becomes two.

Sometimes we cloud our actual motives with a smoke screen of excuses that sound lovely. But there is a huge gap between good sound reasons and reasons that sound good. Often we do this to justify ourselves in the eyes of others.

Rationalization is a mental technique which allows one to be unfair to others without feeling guilty. Rationalization causes people to gloss over open and obvious sin.

So the principle is: If you're wrong in what you are doing, humbly accept correction and stop doing it. No amount of rationalization will make it right or convince anyone else of it being the "right" thing to do. However, should you be sure what you are doing is right and not in any way a contradiction with the word of God and if your conscience is clear then relax and be bold to express yourself with confidence. The main thing is that you please the Lord with a clear conscience.

5. Attitude of Self-Pity

"Self-pity is when you begin to feel that no man's land is your island," said Dana Robins. Self-pity makes you become so absorbed in yourself, you become fascinated by your own ego. In this situation one needs to comprehend that the world was not created for you personally and that it is only your pride and self-centeredness that lies at the root of your problems. Someone once said, "Self-pity is a prison without walls—a sign pointing to nowhere,"

To elude self-pity, you must take your eyes off yourself. When the "I" is put to death, the spirit of Christ can control your life and make it beautiful. Self-pity is as addictive as alcohol—and just as deadly.

Despair and Discouragement

Self-pity is always counter-productive. It is destructive. If continued it will lead to discouragement, which in turn often becomes the most direct route to despair and the ultimate form of self-destruction—suicide. We should not become prisoners of ourselves. When doors are slammed against us, we are prone to draw into ourselves. Distrust begets more distrust. Perhaps some people have lost faith in themselves because they feel God is far away from them. We must trust God even where we cannot trace him.

Deliverance from Depression

The body and the will have their part to play in mastering mental depression. Hence the first step is to get out of whatever situation you find depressing. Some effort on the part of the depressed is necessary. The old maxim, "You never know what you can do until you try," still holds. The ability plus the will to try are the results largely of past efforts that have brought about good results. Surprisingly, time and again we complete tasks which we first thought were beyond our capability. The second step is to look up. We need to look beyond what we can accomplish in our own strength with a positive attitude.

Counter Crisis with Courage

Courage has to be sustained by the encouragement of others. Courage is the keystone in the sustenance of our character. We should have the boldness to stand up for what is right with honesty and justice. In times of crisis we need the attitude of fortitude to keep us from being overcome when things overwhelm us.

God Is Never Off Duty

Hence, the best thing would be to rest in peace, re-evaluate your life and spend your time in prayer and meditation upon the Word of God. Never allow self-pity to overtake you. In essence, self-pity is a bitter resentment of one's condition and an attempt to get back at others or to manipulate others into giving (showing) sympathy.

If you are a person entangled in self-pity, and would like to come out of it, try to do the following: Think about the positive and negative things in your life. Can anything good come out of my illness or my problems? Can I get a much broader and realistic view of the present situation? How can I make the best use of this situation?

There are many such attitudes we should develop. In which areas do we face our greatest struggles? For example are we more often negative than positive? Or are we stubborn and closed rather than open and willing to listen? Are we aloof in our attitude towards others who are different from us? Are we proud and prejudiced? We should dwell on the exhortation of Paul who said, "Have this attitude in yourselves which was also in Christ Jesus,... [who] emptied Himself, taking the form of a bond- servant" (Phil. 2:5,7). May the Lord help us to exercise the attitude of servant-hood as Jesus did.

Therefore, the single most significant decision you can make on a day-to-day basis is your choice of attitude. It is the 'single string' that either keeps you going or cripples your progress. "It alone fuels your desires or assaults your hope," says Charles Swindoll. When your attitudes are right, there is no barrier too high, no valley too deep, no dream too extreme and no challenge too great for you.

9

Faithfulness in Our Prayer Life

The people who have done the most for God are those who have prayed the most. I am sure any person considered to be a great man or woman would definitely be a great prayer warrior in his or her personal life.

ABRAHAM	prayed, his son was born.
ELIEZER	prayed, Rebecca appeared.
JOSEPH	prayed, his brothers were changed.
MOSES	prayed, heaven's wrath was subdued.
JOSHUA	prayed, Ai was destroyed.
HANNAH	prayed, Samuel was gifted.
ELIJAH	prayed, the heavens shut and opened; fire came from above.
ELISHA	prayed, a dead child came back to life.
DAVID	prayed, Goliath was slain.
DANIEL	prayed, the mouths of lions were shut; archangels were set in motion.
JESUS	prayed, the pillars of the church were chosen.
DISCIPLES	prayed, the Holy Spirit came upon them.
THE CHURCH	prayed, Peter released from the prison.

It was PERSISTENT Prayer, PREVAILING Prayer and PINPOINTED Prayer.

What Is Prayer?

Prayer is the declaration of a believer's faith in God and in God's promises. It is an act of expressing our faith in the Lord. The world seeks victory by trying to get back on its feet, but the Christian does it by going down on their knees. Leonard Ravenhill writes, "Poverty-stricken as the church is today in many things, she is most stricken in the place of prayer."

Today many people try to come into the limelight of the spiritual circle but soon they are found like flat tires because there is no backing of prayers in their lives. Often little importance is given to prayer in our churches. There are many organizers, but few agencies; many players, but few prayers; many singers, but few clingers; lots of pastors, but few wrestlers; many fears, but few tears; much fashion, but little passion; many interpreters, but few intercessors; many writers, but few fighters.

The church is becoming poor in terms of prayer. If people are invited to a healing crusade, thousands are likely to come. For an evangelistic meeting, maybe a few hundred would appear, but when someone calls for a prayer meeting, only a scattered few attend. You can commonly hear, "Today, it's only a prayer meeting, not a special gathering." This explains why there is a dearth of spiritual power in our lives. If we had our values right, prayer would be given the greatest and the utmost importance in our schedules.

The current trend in prayer meetings is that we tend to show up with a market list for God. We note many items—a kilo of potatoes, half a kilo of tomatoes, a kilo of rice. etc. You may call it supplication. The Bible says, Go before you're God with "prayer and supplications" (Phil. 4:6).

We make application and then supplications and that is the main part of our prayers. If you happen to record your prayers and play it back, ninety percent of your prayers are about your problems. Often it seems prayers are full of phrases like, "Give me, Lord, give me, give me, give me, I am Jimmy, Lord!" There are many "Give me, I am Jimmy"'s in our spiritual circles. This is not prayer—just supplication.

Prayer is the key that unlocks all the storehouses of God's infinite grace and power. All that God is, and all that God has, is at the disposal of those who pray. There is an unlimited amount of power and authority available with God—but we need to receive it through our earnest prayers. There are no barriers for the believer who knows how to pray and who meets all the conditions of prevailing prayer.

An old Jewish mystic says, "Prayer is the moment when heaven and earth kiss each other." Bring the heavens to come and kiss the earth through your prayers.

The secret of prayer is not what you do or how you do it, for God knows our needs even before we ask. Actually prayer is nothing more than opening up the lines of communication, establishing rapport and removing the roadblocks between God and yourself.

How to Pray So as to Get What You Ask?

One of the most powerful prayers in the Bible is found in Acts 12:5, "But prayer for [Peter] was being made fervently by the church to God." This is the record of a most remarkable prayer. When King Herod killed James, the brother of John, this passage notes that he realized that "it pleased the Jews" (v. 3), so he proceeded to arrest the leader of the whole Apostolic company—the Apostle Peter, intending to kill him as well.

Since this arrest occurred during the Passover week—the holy week of the Jews—even though the Jews were perfectly willing to have Peter assassinated, they were unwilling to have their holy week desecrated by his death. So Peter was cast into prison to be kept until their holy days were over.

On the last night of the Passover week, the eve of the day Peter was supposed to be brought to trial and most likely beheaded, there seemed to be little hope left for Peter's survival. Even so, the Christian believers in Jerusalem held a prayer meeting for Peter. The other disciples and the friends of Peter had gathered in the house of Mary, the mother of John Mark, to make earnest supplication and pray for Peter's release.

They did not attempt any other means or resources to save Peter's life because it all seemed too futile. And what was Peter doing while all this was going on? He was sleeping soundly. Only praying Christians can lay their heads down and sleep soundly at such a time knowing their life is in danger. Besides, there were 16 soldiers standing guard over him—besides the two soldiers who were chained to him on either side. Seeing Peter sleep so peacefully, they too fell asleep.

But then an angel appeared and striking Peter on his side, he woke him up, saying, "Get up quickly."

Maybe Peter's sound sleep came to him because he had prayed something like this: "Lord, no one has any authority over my life. Not a single hair of my head will fall without your permission. If you want me to come to You, I will come. If you want me to stay back, I will stay. My life is in your hands. I hand over my life to you." He was able to say, 'Goodnight, Lord' and sleep because he trusted God implicitly.

We say, "Goodnight, Mummy; goodnight, Daddy; goodnight, darling; goodnight, honey; goodnight, money— and then we go to sleep. But we forget to say, "Goodnight, Lord." If we forget to say "Goodnight, Lord," then at midnight we shouldn't be surprised if Satan comes to say goodnight to us.

If Peter had been worried and did not have faith in the Lord, neither he nor the soldiers would have slept and perhaps the angel might not have come or even if the angel had released him, the soldiers might have been awake and arrested him again.

Many times our worry and disbelief are the hindrances which prevent God from performing miracles in our lives. The Bible asks the rhetorical question: "By worrying are you going to add an inch to your height?" Stop worrying and hand over your problem to the Lord and learn to say, "Lord, this is not my problem it's yours."

The battle is the Lord's, the victory is mine. Perhaps Peter believed this and hence he slept peacefully.

When the angel woke Peter up, the iron chains fell off Peter's hands. Here is another miracle in this passage. We all know that normally when iron chains fall, they make noise. So why did the soldiers not wake at the sound? Because God took care of that. Just as God takes care of every single detail of our problems when we pray and ask God to intervene.

Yet we don't have to tell God, "Be careful when you are performing that miracle, because the iron chains are going to make a noise." God knows already. Some folk try to elaborate and explain their petitions to God regarding what they want. All we really have to do with our prayer requests is just to relax and hand over the entire problem to the Lord. Many times as soon as we finish praying, we try to manipulate the situation which precludes allowing God to do a miracle on our behalf.

The story of Peter's miraculous release from his prison chains continues with a description of his arrival at the house of Mary, mother of Mark. Peter most likely knew intercessions were being made at this house of prayer and that his fellow believers would be praying for him. When he knocked at the door, a servant girl named Rhoda, who was praying along with others, went to see who was at the door. She might have thought it was a late arrival to the prayer session, but when she recognized Peter's voice she became so excited she forgot to open the door, dashing back to tell the group about Peter's arrival.

Everyone was incredulous and virtually stunned, so Peter kept knocking until someone finally opened the door and there he was! Peter stood at the doorstep, as a living evidence of God's answer to their prayer.

It is amazing to notice that, besides Mary's name, whose house it was, among all the rest of the praying disciples, only Rhoda, the lowly servant girl, was mentioned by name in Scriptures. Rhoda means "rose" and surely her faith was a lovely fragrance to God. There is no sweeter fragrance to God than the fragrance of faith.

In contemplating how these people prayed, we note: "prayer for him was being made fervently by the church to God." The whole secret of prevailing prayer is found in four phrases in this brief description of their uttered prayer: (i) "to God"; (ii) "fervently"; (iii) "the church"; (iv) "for him."

Let us now analyze these items one by one.

Praying unto God

What do we mean by praying "unto God"? Why does it say here that they prayed "unto God"? Don't we all pray to God? Praying "unto God" means, I believe, entering into the presence of God and praying.

Often when people stand up to pray in public or kneel down in private closets, they tend to think far more of what they ask for, but fail to contemplate the greatness of God who made heaven and earth and who possesses power over all things. We do lip service to the name of God, but there is no real conscious access to God. If we really want our prayers to be powerful, the first step is to experience the presence of God while we pray.

Brother Lawrence once said, "Prayer is nothing else than a sense of God's presence." In order to achieve this state of concentration, we need to forget and forsake everything around us and remain silently before God until we feel God's presence.

The best time to pray is early in the morning. The Lord promises that the one who seeks God early shall find the Lord. So get up early in the morning and pray.

What should you do early in the morning? Get up! Some don't like to get up, but prefer lying down to have a horizontal meditation. They pray, "Lord, thank you for the night's sleep and the rest you gave me," and then they snore back to sleep and when they wake up again, they resume their prayers.

No horizontal meditation will do. Amos says, "Woe to those who are at ease in Zion" (6:1). There's no real rest for Christians. If you rest, you will rust. Get up from your bed, go through your morning ablutions so you don't approach God with bad breath.

Feel refreshed as you approach the Lord. If the president of your country calls you tonight to come for dinner, how would you go? Of course you would have on your best outfit, a suitable hairstyle, the best perfume possible and you would be fresh and clean. If you can go to a worldly authority this well prepared, how should you approach the presence of the Lord of Lords and the King of Kings.

We Christians often have no fear of God. We take the love of God for granted. Adherents of other religions seem to have more fear of their gods than we Christians do. I suspect

Christians don't fear Jesus because our Lord is not portrayed holding a spear or a sword in His hand. Yet Scriptures warn us that we are to approach our God with fear and trembling. If we do that, then we can stand before others reflecting the power and authority that only comes from God. So the presence of God is most important.

There are two important spiritual disciplines that we need to cultivate: (1) Do not start praying unless you have felt the presence of God. (2) Whenever you open the Bible never close it without allowing God to speak to you— because it is God's Word and it will not return back to you void. God definitely has something to say to you from the portion you are reading, but you must wait patiently in God's presence to listen to the Lord's voice. Christian life is a life of discipline. The word "disciple" comes from the word "discipline". And discipline pays dividends.

People are in a hurry to pray quickly and go to work or do other things. Someone once prayed: "God bless me, my wife, my son and my daughter; we four and no more." It is not we four and no more. Never be in a hurry when you pray. Do you hurry up when you watch your favorite sport being played? In the middle of the game you don't say "One, two and I'm going away now." You are sure to relax and watch to the end of the game.

We all need to relax and pray—and wait for the

presence of God. If God's presence seems remote, read a few verses of the Psalms or Proverbs, or sing a few songs of praise. Surely these will help you feel the presence of God. Sit there in quiet meditation until you feel the presence of God—and then start praying.

Make it a discipline (practice) in your life that you will not start praying if you are unable to feel the presence of God. Rather start by crying out, "Lord, what is that is hindering You from coming to me? What barrier exists between You and me? Why am I not able to feel Your presence." Cry to the Lord and now perhaps God will remind you of how you scolded your spouse so that the two of you slept on opposite sides of the bed without reconciling with one another—and now, this morning you expect you gloss this over and enter the Lord's presence as though nothing were wrong? Absolutely not! The Lord reminds you, "I'm not a cheap God. Go say you're sorry to your spouse and then come to Me."

Or have you been watching obscene movies on television or on the internet which has led you into all sorts of fantasies and hallucinations so now your mind is in a mess? Do you expect God just to appear as soon as you start praying? Of course not. Our God is a holy God. The author of Hebrews warns us that without holiness, no one will see the Lord (12:14).

You think that just because you are praying, your prayers are being heard. No, it does not just happen. First comes the conviction through the Holy Spirit of any unconfessed sin in our hearts. Then comes the confession—which is not just telling God you have sinned. The Lord already knows and that is why God has given you that conviction.

Rather confession means agreeing with God and saying, "Yes, Lord, I have sinned." Then comes the cleansing through the blood of Jesus which results in the renewed communion with God. These four C's are very important: the Conviction, the Confession, the Cleansing and the Communion with God.

Once the confession is taken care of, you can be assured of God's presence and know that your prayers will now get into the computer of God and you can be certain of getting an output. This is what is meant by going into the presence of God.

But we must remember we can only access the presence of God through our Lord Jesus Christ! (Eph. 2:18) What happens when we come into the presence of God? The woman who approached Jesus in Luke 7:37-38 is a good model. When she came into the Lord's presence she did not even utter a word for her heart was completely broken. This incident stands as a model for us to come into the presence of God with a contrite heart and a need to empty ourselves at Christ's feet.

Remember, the Lord does not despise a broken heart and a remorseful spirit. If you go to God with a proud heart, the Lord can never fill you with His grace and peace. God can only fill an empty and clean vessel—not one that is half-filled. Go before the Lord with a broken spirit, empty yourself, humble yourself, prostrate yourself before the living God—as this humble woman came into Christ's presence—broken.

She knew not how to pray or ask for help. She never opened her mouth or uttered a word, but her tears were eloquent and they also washed the feet of Jesus. Every teardrop was a confession of every sin in her life. She did not know how to pray but she knew how to be broken at the feet of Jesus— which is how you go into the Lord's presence. God is the only one who looks at your heart and not at your worldly possessions.

No matter how bleak your situation might appear, I want to tell you, 'Cheer up! The Lord is at work.' You may not see

anything but darkness, but you are praying. If you love God you must rest in the fact that the Lord loves you too—for God is love. The Lord has obviously started working in your life and soon you will see the light appear. When the dawn comes you will see what the Lord has been doing in your life.

The disciples were praying in a room across town, but the iron chains that bound Peter broke and fell off him— without waking the guards. Is it not a miracle? The same miracle will happen as the shackles of sin fall away from your life.

Pray Without Ceasing

Now let us consider the second phrase of the four used in Acts 12:5, that contains the secret of prevailing prayer. The phrase "without ceasing" is translated from the Greek word *ektenos* which means "stretched-out-edly." It is the same word used in Luke 22:44 for "being in agony" when Jesus was praying fervently and His sweat appeared as drops of blood falling upon the ground. The simile that comes to mind is that our spirits are being stretched out toward God in intense earnestness of desire—or like the pouring out of oneself on the altar of God.

Pray United in One Spirit

The third of these four phrases, "of the church," implies a united presence. Our prayers together delight God. There is, of course, power in the prayer of a single individual, but there is far greater power in united prayer. Matthew's gospel describes our Lord Jesus teaching this great truth": "Truly I say to you, whatever you bind on earth shall have been bound in heaven; and whatever you loose on earth shall have been loosed in heaven... If two of you agree on earth..." (18:19-19).

There is power in united prayer—provided there is real unity. There should be oneness in the body of Christ—the believers. There should not be differences or hatred or unforgiving spirits or jealousy among believers. If there is no unity there can be no power in prayer.

Pray Specific, Particular Prayers

The fourth phrase, "for him," denotes that this offered prayer was a definite one—for a definite person. This is the kind of prayer God answers specifically. "General prayers are generally heard." God's answer is just as definite as your prayer is. While both Peter and Paul were imprisoned, Peter had a sound sleep and Paul sang in high spirits. The former was peaceful and the latter joyful. They had learned to relax and rejoice, even in depressing and difficult situations. Peter knew Whom he had trusted and Paul knew Whom he had tasted (1 Pet. 2:3; 2 Tim. 1:12).

In summing this up, we need to understand our dependence upon the Holy Spirit in all our praying. It is the Holy Spirit who enables us to really approach God in spirit and in truth. The Spirit leads us into God's presence and makes God real to us. Again it is the Holy Spirit who gives us the intense earnestness in prayer that prevails with God and Who brings us into unity so we know the power of united prayer. The Holy Spirit confirms in our heart those things for which we should definitely pray.

To sum up, we must remember that the prayer God answers is the prayer offered to the Father, on the ground of the atoning blood of the Son, under the direction and in the power of the Holy Spirit.

10

Faithfulness of a Firewood Christian

Everything that touches humans concern the church. The modern church succumbs to the worldly pattern by allowing secular thinking to reduce it to a specialized fellowship of worship rather than being a committed community shaped by its life in Christ. Today our churches do not reflect Jesus and therefore do not interpret him. Someone once said, "It is not our claim, as the truth which is absolute, but the claim of the truth on us." The church cannot incarnate God, unless it is willing to go to the cross, to walk an extra mile, emptying itself of all pretensions in the ultimate sacrifice which alone makes its incarnation convincing.

1. Upper Room or Supper Room

We need to learn much from the Early Church. Someone commented, "The Early Church prayed in the Upper Room, but the present church cooks in the supper room." Much time is given for playing and feasting rather than fasting and praying. We see more people with full stomachs but not with broken hearts, bent knees and wet eyes. There is more fire in the kitchen range than in the pulpit.

The Early Church was filled with the Holy Ghost, not stuffed with stew and roast. Shall we put out the cooking squad and bring in the praying band, spend less time cooking and more time meditating on the Book. Let us have fewer dinners but win more sinners. The trouble with many Christians today is that they would rather be on the judgment seat than on the witness stand.

2. Ideologies or Theology

The church at present is a broken sign, divided not only by doctrinal controversies but also by the same forces of class, color and creed that split the human community. It finds itself in a situation analogous to its early days in the Roman Empire, confronting powerful ideologies beyond its own boundaries. Today we are troubled less by golden calves than by graven image theologies.

3. The Church That Cares

The greatest need today is for a church that cares, that heals the lives that are hurt, that comforts old people, that challenges the youth, that knows no division of culture or caste, no frontiers—geographical or social. It should be a working church, a worshipping church and a winsome church. It should also be a church that interprets the truth in terms of the truth.

4. The Church on Fire

Today in our churches God wants men and women who are on fire. Our God himself is a consuming fire (Heb. 12:29). Samuel Pringle gave this incredible definition of fire: "It is love; it is faith; it is hope; it is divine discontent with formality, ceremonialism, lukewarmness and indifference." It is this fire that is missing in our churches. A cold church is like cold butter—it never spreads very well.

a) Firewood Christians

If the church is to be on fire, every member of the church need be firewood. The Holy Spirit of God can ignite such firewood to burn for the Lord's glory. But how can we become firewood for Christ?

First the tree has to be cut from the earth, so our roots in the world must be cut off and plucked out of its surroundings. Then the tree is cut into pieces, and so we must allow the Lord to cut us and shape us according to the Lord's purpose. God will see us through testing or through pain and suffering. Then these pieces of cut-up wood must be dried in the hot sun—which is analogous to our being dried in the hot sun of patience which thus prepares us to burn brightly for our Lord. But these prepared pieces are not immediately used in the stove or furnace. They are piled as stock in a handy place so they can be used in the appointed time.

The church or our ministry can be compared to the stove or furnace. According to the Lord's time and purpose God takes us into His church or ministry so that we may burn for Him. This required us to wait patiently in prayer and preparation in the place where God has put us until He leads us to a specific place and ministry. If the firewood starts burning where it is stockpiled or even before when it is still growing in the forest, it will cause destruction.

b) Burning Christians

Firewood does not burn by itself. It only starts burning when it is touched by fire. The Holy Spirit must touch us, fill us and anoint us with holy fire so we might start burning for Christ. If the wood has not been properly dried it will produce a lot of smoke—causing many tears. Many Christians and ministers appear to try to burn for Christ before they are prepared properly—knowing the Lord and the Word of God. As such they become a hindrance to the kingdom of God.

When Jesus Christ becomes for us the best news, then we will become messengers of the good news. If we are still enmeshed in the world, we would only be smokey Christians, and others would easily judge us as immature or an unprepared witnesses for Christ. Hence we must have lives totally surrendered to Christ and be filled with the Holy Spirit before we can be fuel for the Lord. Paul says, "Be filled with the Spirit" (Eph. 5:18) which is a present, continuous tense. So we must have an ongoing filling of the Spirit to be fuel for God's use. It is easy to light a fire, but without fuel it will not continue to burn.

c) United Christian

A solitary piece of firewood burning by itself soon dies out. Burning alongside two or three other pieces, it will burn brighter and longer. So we, too, must unite with others and minister in one spirit if we are to have an effective ministry. King Solomon wisely said, "Two are better than one because they have a good return for their labor.... And if one can overpower him who is alone, two can resist him. A cord of three strands is not quickly torn apart" (Ecc. 4:9-12).

This passage points out four significant benefits derived for those who minister together. Mutual effort produces a good return for your labor (v. 9). Through mutual support we can lift one another up (v. 10). Mutual encouragement helps us boldly face threatening times (v. 11). Through mutual strength we can resist attackers (v. 12).

d) Charcoal Christians

Good firewood will turn into charcoal after burning. It can still be used as a fuel though not to the extent as the original firewood. So, even if we become old, we can still burn in the ministry of prayer and intercession, in counseling and writing as well. Charcoal can be used until it becomes fine ash and then it flies away in thin air. Likewise God can use us until our last breath and we are promoted to the heavenly kingdom.

5. Fire and Mission

"The church exists by mission as fire exists by burning," said Emil Brunner. Firewood is not concerned with what is kept on the stove. It may be plain water or simple rice, an exotic fish curry or a tasty roast chicken. The firewood keeps burning irrespective of the purpose for which it is utilized.

Likewise all of us who are believers must be willing and enabled to proclaim the gospel and make disciples that will be called into the one body of Christ—a community and a fellowship which binds people in loving interdependence, irrespective of the worldly barriers of denominations, social status, race, color or nationality. We are called to leave off being mere spectators to become active participants in church ministry.

Irrespective of the type of ministry or its application,

we must be totally surrendered to the cause of proclaiming Christ, without any conditions or reservations—like the firewood burning inside the stove. When the Lord becomes the center of our undivided attention and devotion, the success and fruit of our ministry will move from being a distant dream to being an obtainable reality.

Paul explains in Ephesians 2 that Christ is the One who, through his death, made it possible for diverse people to come together as spiritual brothers and sisters (v. 11-22). Spiritual and relational oneness does not always coexist. Although we may be bound together by one Savior, we do not automatically serve one another in love and respect as family members.

A prime example of this unity is found in Joshua for we read how an essential element of the success of the Israelites was their willingness to tackle their God-given task together. Without resistance, they accepted an unusual strategy for the conquest of Jericho. By standing united in obedience to God and his chosen leader, they became an invincible force through which the Lord could carry out his work—and get all the praise and glory.

Without jealousy, the Israelites worked as a team to accomplish their God-given objectives. Without doubting, they trusted the Lord and their leaders—and they were rewarded. As a united people with a single objective, they stood as a formidable and fearsome force.

May the Lord help us to yield our lives into the total control of the Holy Spirit so we might burn for Christ until the end of our days.

11

Faithfulness in Our Character

A scorpion, being a poor swimmer, asked a turtle to carry him on his back across a river. "Are you mad?" exclaimed the turtle. "You will sting me while I'm swimming and I'll drown."

"My dear turtle," laughed the scorpion. "If I were to sting you, you would drown and I would go down with you. Now, where is the logic in that?"

"You're right," said the turtle. "Hop on!"

The scorpion climbed aboard and halfway across the river it gave the turtle a mighty sting. As they both sank to the bottom, the turtle said, "Do you mind if I ask you something? You said there'd be no logic in you stinging me. Why then did you do it?"

"It has nothing to do with logic," the drowning scorpion sadly replied. "It's just my character."

Character is that part of a person that makes them different from others. Character—being the crown and glory of life—lies in the will of a person. It is a habit long continued but also it is our noblest possession. "A man of character will make himself worthy of any position he is given," said Mahatma Gandhi.

So, it is not what we do for God that counts, but what we are before the Lord that matters. What we are determines the value of what we say and do. As a sage once commented, "Unless there is within us that which is above, we shall soon yield to that which is around us."

Charismatic leaders have attractive personalities. Charisma is not necessarily flamboyance, loudness, or dynamism. It may also be a meek and quiet spirit in the midst of a sea of boastful commercialism and slick advertising. A pocket watch and a public clock both serve the same purpose—to tell the time. If a watch goes out of order, only the owner is affected; but if a public clock goes wrong hundreds of people are misled. So, as responsible citizens of this country, let us be examples and let not our lives be a stumbling block to others.

Peter Kusmic has said, "Charisma without character is catastrophe." The circumstances amid which we live determine our reputation; the truth we believe determines our character.

1. Reputation Versus Character

Reputation is what we are supposed to be. Character is what we are.

Reputation is the photograph. Character is the face. Reputation is earned in a moment. Character is built through

a lifetime. Reputation is what others put on our tombstone. Character is what angels say about us before the throne of God. Reputation is sometimes as wide as the horizon but character is the point of needle. A person's reputation comes from our behavior in public, but character is what we do when we know no one will ever find out.

2. Character and Integrity

Integrity is what we gain by walking in God's light. It is worth far more than precious gold to do what is true and right. Integrity is a state or quality of being complete. It is the integration of a personality. In spite of severe persecution and discouragement, Job held onto his integrity. He said, "Till I die I will not put away my integrity."

A good test of our character is our behavior when we make mistakes. No one goes crooked as long as we stay on the straight and narrow path. Our character is shaped by what our minds take in; we should not be like a wastepaper basket. We are more than a sum of what happens to us. Character evolves through our beliefs, our attitudes, our intentions and our motives. Our reasons do not count as the real "explanation" of our behavior. We can easily judge the character of a person by observing how they treat those who can do nothing for them or to them.

3. Choices and Character

Choice is the starting point of action; it is source of motion but not the end for the sake of which we act. Little choices determine habit. Habits carve and mold character.

Why Do Even Those of Great Reputation Fall?

Any of us can fall if our intentions are to act contrary to our basic convictions or to the moral principles of God— especially if our judgment has been clouded by "desire" or overwhelmed by "passion." We develop character through our concrete decisions—which in turn determines our destiny. Circumstances do not make a person, they only reveal what they are made of.

Theodore H. Epp said, "Lust is the bud, sin is the blossom, and death is the fruit." That is why it is important to nip temptation in the bud before it can blossom into sin and death. David was a great man but sin defeated him. The Bible says, "Therefore let him who thinks he stands take heed that he does not fall" (1 Cor. 10:12).

You may wonder, "Can a thing like this possibly happen to me?" Yes it can. In some unguarded moment, Satan can slip up on your weak side and set before you a temptation so alluring that in your own strength you'll be unable to overcome it. Our trouble is not that we are tempted, but that we don't turn to God for deliverance, but rather turn to someone else for counseling when the temptation is before us.

4. Courage Sustains Character

Courage needs to be sustained by the encouragement of others. Courage is the keystone in the sustenance of our character. We should have the boldness to stand for what is right and be honest and just. In times of crisis we need the attitude of fortitude to keep us from being overcome when things run over us.

In the Bible we find evidence of God using trials to refine Paul's character. Paul even learned to rejoice in his sufferings because he found that suffering produced endurance, which in turn produced character, and then character produced hope.

Character is what we are in the dark. We can sell our character but we cannot purchase it. The hardest trial of our character is whether we can bear a rival's failure without triumph. We show our character by what makes us laugh.

In the destiny of every moral being, there is an object considered more worthy by God than anything else—that is our character. It exercises a greater power over us than wealth and secures all honor without pining for fame. It carries with it an influence and commands the general confidence and respect of others.

Keeping character is easier than recovering it. Character is made by many acts; but a single one can lose it. The toughest thing in life is to remove the stains from our character. "Character is like a tree and reputation is like its shadow. The shadow is what we think of it; the tree is the real thing," said Abraham Lincoln.

The fragrance of our rich and delightful character will continue to linger about the place where we lived, as a dried rose bud scents the drawer where it has withered and perished. Purity in your heart produces power in your life. Righteousness produces beauty in your character. Do what you can, where you are, with what you have.

Additional copies of this book may be obtained
from your bookstore
or by contacting
Hope Publishing House
P.O. Box 60008
Pasadena, CA 91116 - U.S.A.
(626) 792-6123 / Fax (626) 792-2121
HopePublishingHouse@gmail.com
www.hope-pub.com